I0012074

Mastering AutoGPT:

A Professional's Guide to Autonomous AI Agents

Introduction

rtificial Intelligence (AI) has entered a new era with the advent of autonomous agents like AutoGPT. No longer limited to simple task execution, these AI-driven systems can think, plan, and iterate on their objectives with minimal human oversight. Powered by large language models (LLMs), AutoGPT is capable of breaking down complex problems, formulating strategies, and adapting its approach to optimize results.

This guide is designed for professionals seeking a deep understanding of AutoGPT's capabilities, architecture, and practical applications. Whether you're an entrepreneur looking to streamline business operations, a researcher exploring AI-driven automation, or a developer aiming to integrate AutoGPT into your workflow, this book will provide you with the knowledge and tools to harness its full potential. Through detailed explanations, real-world use cases, and step-by-step deployment strategies, you'll gain the expertise needed to implement AutoGPT effectively and unlock new levels of productivity and innovation.

Let's dive into the future of autonomous AI and explore how AutoGPT can revolutionize the way we work and solve problems.

Chapter 1: What is AutoGPT?

Artificial Intelligence (AI) has rapidly evolved from rule-based systems to sophisticated machine learning models capable of understanding, reasoning, and executing complex tasks. Among the latest innovations in AI is **AutoGPT**, an autonomous AI agent that pushes the boundaries of traditional large language models (LLMs) by independently strategizing, planning, and executing tasks with minimal human intervention.

This chapter provides a foundational understanding of AutoGPT, highlighting its core principles, key differentiators from other AI models, and its practical applications for professionals.

1.1 The Concept of Autonomous AI Agents

Traditional AI Models vs. Autonomous AI

Historically, AI models have been designed as reactive systems—responding to user inputs but lacking independent decision-making abilities. Traditional AI models, such as ChatGPT, require continuous prompts and guidance from humans to generate outputs. While they excel at natural language processing (NLP) and content generation, they do not possess autonomy, memory, or the ability to work iteratively on a given task.

Autonomous AI agents, like AutoGPT, represent a paradigm shift. Instead of functioning as passive responders, they proactively define goals, break down tasks into actionable steps, and continuously refine their outputs based on feedback. This ability allows them to complete complex workflows with minimal supervision, making them invaluable in professional settings where efficiency and scalability are critical.

How AutoGPT Differs from ChatGPT and Other LLM-Based Models

AutoGPT builds upon the capabilities of ChatGPT and similar LLMs but introduces several fundamental enhancements:

1. **Goal-Oriented Execution** – Unlike ChatGPT, which provides responses based on individual prompts, AutoGPT can set long-term objectives and decompose them into smaller tasks that it executes systematically.
2. **Self-Iteration and Refinement** – AutoGPT can assess its own outputs, make adjustments, and iterate until it achieves the best possible result.
3. **Memory Utilization** – It retains contextual information across tasks, allowing for improved consistency and decision-making over extended workflows.
4. **Multi-Agent Collaboration** – AutoGPT can coordinate multiple AI agents, assigning them specialized tasks and integrating their outputs for seamless execution.

By combining these capabilities, AutoGPT transcends traditional AI limitations and unlocks new possibilities for automation and problem-solving.

1.2 Key Features of AutoGPT

1. Goal-Oriented Processing

AutoGPT operates based on clearly defined objectives. Instead of requiring explicit step-by-step instructions, it autonomously determines the best approach to achieving a given goal. This makes it ideal for handling complex projects that require planning, execution, and optimization without human intervention at every stage.

2. Memory Utilization for Task Continuity

Unlike standard LLMs, which treat each interaction as isolated, AutoGPT leverages memory to store previous interactions, task progress, and contextual knowledge. This allows it to maintain consistency across multi-step processes, reducing redundancy and improving efficiency.

3. Iterative Learning and Improvement

One of AutoGPT's most powerful capabilities is its ability to refine its own outputs. It can analyze its results, identify errors or inefficiencies, and make necessary adjustments. This iterative approach enables it to continuously improve the quality and accuracy of its work, mimicking human problem-solving strategies.

4. Multi-Agent Collaboration

AutoGPT can function as a **team of AI agents**, where different instances work together to complete various aspects of a project. For example, in a software development task, one agent can handle code generation, another can test and debug, while a third compiles documentation. This multi-agent approach enhances productivity and enables complex, multi-faceted workflows.

1.3 Use Cases for Professionals

AutoGPT's advanced capabilities make it a valuable tool for professionals across various industries. Below are some of the most impactful use cases:

1. Business Automation

AutoGPT can streamline operations by automating repetitive and time-consuming tasks such as:

- Customer support via AI-powered chatbots
- Email drafting and scheduling
- Financial report generation
- Market research and competitor analysis

By automating these processes, businesses can significantly reduce operational costs and improve efficiency.

2. Data Analysis and Reporting

Professionals dealing with large datasets can use AutoGPT to:

- Collect, clean, and analyze data

- Identify trends and generate visual reports
- Automate real-time monitoring and insights
- Generate executive summaries based on data interpretations

This capability is particularly useful for analysts, financial professionals, and researchers who need fast and accurate data-driven insights.

3. Code Generation and Debugging

Developers can leverage AutoGPT to:

- Write and optimize code in various programming languages
- Detect and fix bugs in existing software
- Generate detailed documentation and API references
- Assist in learning new programming frameworks and best practices

AutoGPT significantly accelerates software development, reducing human workload and improving code quality.

4. Research and Content Creation

Writers, academics, and marketers can use AutoGPT for:

- Generating high-quality articles, reports, and whitepapers
- Summarizing complex research papers
- Conducting literature reviews and gathering references
- Creating SEO-optimized content for digital marketing

By automating research and content generation, professionals can save time while ensuring high-quality outputs.

5. AI-Driven Project Management

Project managers and executives can integrate AutoGPT into their workflows to:

- Automate task allocation and scheduling
- Generate project roadmaps and risk assessments
- Track progress and suggest optimizations

- Provide real-time status updates and decision-making support

This makes project execution more streamlined, ensuring efficiency and goal alignment.

Conclusion

AutoGPT represents a breakthrough in AI-driven automation, transforming the way professionals work by offering goal-oriented execution, iterative learning, and multi-agent collaboration. By understanding its capabilities and potential applications, professionals can leverage AutoGPT to enhance productivity, improve decision-making, and unlock new opportunities in their respective fields.

Chapter 2: Setting Up AutoGPT

AutoGPT is a powerful autonomous AI agent capable of executing complex tasks with minimal human intervention. However, to harness its full potential, proper setup and configuration are crucial. This chapter provides a step-by-step guide to installing AutoGPT, configuring it for various use cases, and optimizing its performance based on specific needs.

2.1 Prerequisites

Before installing AutoGPT, you need to ensure that your system meets the required dependencies. Below are the key prerequisites for setting up and running AutoGPT.

1. Python Installation

AutoGPT is built using Python, so having the correct version installed is essential.

Checking if Python is Installed

Open a terminal or command prompt and run:

bash

```
python --version
```

or

bash

```
python3 --version
```

If Python is installed, you will see output similar to:

bash

```
Python 3.x.x
```

AutoGPT requires **Python 3.8 or higher**. If you have an older version, update Python by downloading the latest version from the official website: <u>Download Python</u>

After installation, verify again using the command:

bash

```
python3 --version
```

2. OpenAI API Key

AutoGPT relies on OpenAI's API to access large language models (LLMs) such as GPT-4. To use the API, you need an API key.

Steps to Obtain an OpenAI API Key:

1. Go to OpenAI's API page.
2. Sign up or log in to your OpenAI account.
3. Navigate to the API section and generate a new API key.
4. Copy and securely store your API key, as it will be required for AutoGPT's configuration.

Tip: Avoid sharing your API key or exposing it in public repositories.

3. Dependencies and Libraries

AutoGPT requires several dependencies to function properly, including:

- **LangChain** – for handling AI agents and memory

- **Pinecone** (optional) – for long-term memory storage
- **Tiktoken** – for token management
- **OpenAI API client** – for model interaction
- **Other standard Python libraries**

To install these dependencies, run:

bash

```
pip install -r requirements.txt
```

If the file is unavailable, manually install the required libraries:

bash

```
pip install openai langchain pinecone-client tiktoken
```

2.2 Installation Guide

Once you have the prerequisites set up, follow this guide to install AutoGPT.

1. Clone the AutoGPT Repository

Navigate to the directory where you want to install AutoGPT and clone the official repository:

bash

```
git clone https://github.com/Torantulino/Auto-GPT.git
cd Auto-GPT
```

2. Install Required Dependencies

Run the following command to install all necessary dependencies:

bash

```
pip install -r requirements.txt
```

3. Configure API Access

AutoGPT requires your OpenAI API key to function. Open the .env.template file and rename it to .env:

bash

```
mv .env.template .env
```

Then, open the .env file in a text editor and update the OPENAI_API_KEY field:

bash

OPENAI_API_KEY=your_openai_api_key_here

Save and close the file.

4. Setting Up Local vs. Cloud Deployment

AutoGPT can run either **locally** or in the **cloud**, depending on your needs.

Local Deployment

Running AutoGPT locally ensures complete control over data privacy but requires significant computational power, especially for memory-intensive tasks.

To run AutoGPT locally, simply execute:

bash

```
python -m autogpt
```

Cloud Deployment (Optional)

For users requiring high scalability, AutoGPT can be deployed in the cloud using platforms like **AWS, Google Cloud, or Azure**.

For **Docker-based cloud deployment**, first, install Docker and then use the following command to build and run AutoGPT in a container:

bash

```
docker build -t autogpt .
docker run -d autogpt
```

2.3 Configuring AutoGPT for Your Needs

Once AutoGPT is installed, it's essential to customize it for optimal performance based on specific tasks and objectives.

1. Customizing Goals and Constraints

AutoGPT operates based on predefined **goals** and **constraints**. These define what the AI should achieve and the boundaries within which it must operate.

Defining Goals

To specify goals, modify the ai_settings.yaml file:

yaml

```
ai_name: "ResearchAssistant"
ai_role: "An AI that conducts in-depth market research and compiles reports."
ai_goals:
  - "Analyze market trends and provide a detailed report."
  - "Identify potential investment opportunities."
  - "Summarize competitor strategies."
```

Each goal should be **clear, measurable, and achievable**.

Setting Constraints

Constraints define AutoGPT's limitations to ensure responsible AI behavior. For example:

yaml

```yaml
ai_constraints:
  - "Do not access restricted data."
  - "Avoid excessive API calls."
  - "Ensure outputs are under 1000 words."
```

2. Enabling Memory Storage

By default, AutoGPT runs in a stateless mode, meaning it doesn't retain past interactions. Enabling memory allows it to **remember previous conversations and improve responses over time**.

Using Pinecone for Long-Term Memory

To enable Pinecone, update the .env file with the following details:

bash

```bash
PINECONE_API_KEY=your_pinecone_api_key
PINECONE_ENV=us-west1-gcp
```

Alternatively, for a local memory store, modify the memory_backend setting:

yaml

memory_backend: "local"

Tip: If running AutoGPT locally, ensure sufficient storage and processing power for memory-intensive tasks.

3. Managing Task Execution Parameters

Fine-tuning execution settings allows AutoGPT to optimize performance based on task complexity.

Adjusting Execution Speed

Modify the config.json file to control execution parameters:

json

```
{
  "fast_mode": true,
  "max_iterations": 5,
  "execution_speed": "balanced"
}
```

- "fast_mode": true – Enables rapid processing.
- "max_iterations": 5 – Limits task iterations to optimize performance.

- "execution_speed": "balanced" — Adjusts between speed and accuracy.

Managing API Call Limits

To prevent excessive API usage, set a maximum token usage per task:

yaml

max_tokens: 4000

Tip: Reducing max tokens conserves API costs while maintaining efficiency.

Conclusion

Setting up AutoGPT requires installing the necessary dependencies, configuring API access, and fine-tuning parameters based on specific goals. Whether deploying locally or in the cloud, careful customization ensures optimal performance.

Chapter 3: How AutoGPT Works Under the Hood

AutoGPT is not just a simple AI chatbot—it is an autonomous agent capable of planning, executing, and refining tasks with minimal human intervention. Understanding its internal workings will help professionals optimize its performance for various applications.

In this chapter, we will break down how AutoGPT:
- Plans and executes tasks efficiently.
- Uses memory to retain context.
- Coordinates multiple agents for complex problem-solving.

3.1 Task Planning and Execution

At the core of AutoGPT's intelligence lies its ability to **break down objectives into actionable steps**, execute them recursively, and optimize outcomes through a feedback loop.

1. How AutoGPT Breaks Down Objectives

Unlike traditional AI models that rely on user prompts for every interaction, AutoGPT is designed to work autonomously by following a structured approach:

1-**Understanding the goal** – AutoGPT first analyzes the given objective and determines what needs to be accomplished.

2-**Task decomposition** – It breaks the goal into **smaller, manageable subtasks** to improve efficiency.

3-**Prioritization** – The AI prioritizes subtasks based on dependencies, urgency, and logical order.

4-**Execution** – AutoGPT processes each task sequentially or in parallel, depending on its complexity.

Example: Suppose the goal is to **"Research the latest AI advancements and summarize key trends."** AutoGPT will decompose this into:

- Identify reliable AI research sources.

- Extract relevant publications from the past 12 months.
- Analyze key themes in AI development.
- Summarize findings into a report.

2. Recursive Task Execution

AutoGPT employs **recursive reasoning**, meaning it can:

- Re-evaluate its approach if a task fails.
- Modify its execution plan based on results.
- Iterate over subtasks until the objective is met.

This makes it vastly superior to static AI models, which rely on single-shot responses.

Example: If AutoGPT is asked to generate a Python script but encounters an error, it will:
- Debug the issue.
- Rewrite problematic sections.
- Test the script again.
- Only finalize the output when it meets the expected criteria.

3. Feedback Loop Optimization

AutoGPT continuously improves its outputs through a **feedback loop**:

1. **Self-evaluation** – After completing a task, it assesses whether the output meets predefined success criteria.
2. **Refinement** – If the result is unsatisfactory, it refines its approach and reattempts the task.
3. **User validation (optional)** – In some cases, AutoGPT may request user confirmation before proceeding.

Use Case: In business automation, AutoGPT can analyze marketing trends, generate reports, and refine strategies by iterating over data until meaningful insights emerge.

3.2 Memory and Context Retention

For an AI to function autonomously, it must **remember previous interactions**. AutoGPT achieves this using **short-term and long-term memory storage**.

1. Short-Term vs. Long-Term Memory

Memory Type	Function	Use Case
Short-Term Memory (STM)	Stores temporary data for immediate tasks.	Holding conversation context within a session.
Long-Term Memory (LTM)	Retains information across multiple interactions.	Remembering user preferences over weeks or months.

Example:

If you ask AutoGPT to write a series of articles, **short-term memory** ensures continuity within the same session, while **long-term memory** allows it to maintain consistency across multiple sessions.

2. Database Integrations (Vector Databases)

AutoGPT uses **vector databases** to store and retrieve memory efficiently. Some common integrations include:

- **Pinecone** – Optimized for high-speed vector searches.
- **Weaviate** – Offers hybrid search capabilities.
- **FAISS (Facebook AI Similarity Search)** – Used for large-scale memory storage.

When a user interacts with AutoGPT, the system queries the vector database to **retrieve relevant past interactions** before generating a response.

3. Strategies for Improving Memory Efficiency

To optimize AutoGPT's memory performance, consider the following:

- **Set memory limits** – Avoid unnecessary storage of low-priority data.
- **Use summarization techniques** – Store condensed versions of interactions instead of full conversations.

- **Choose the right database** – Select a vector database that aligns with your performance needs.

Use Case: A business analyst using AutoGPT for financial forecasting can configure long-term memory to **track economic trends over time**, leading to more informed predictions.

3.3 Multi-Agent Coordination

AutoGPT is not limited to a single instance—it can run **multiple agents in parallel**, each handling different aspects of a complex task.

1. How Multiple Instances Interact

Multi-agent systems allow for **task delegation**, where different AI instances specialize in:

Data analysis

Content generation

Software automation

Decision-making

Each agent can **share data** with others to ensure seamless collaboration.

 Example:

An AI-driven **customer support** system might include:

- One agent handling FAQs.

- Another analyzing customer sentiment.

- A third escalating critical issues to a human operator.

2. Role-Based Agent Tasks

To enhance efficiency, AutoGPT can assign specific **roles** to different agents:

Agent Type	Primary Function	Example
Planner Agent	Breaks down complex objectives.	"Create a business expansion strategy."
Research Agent	Gathers and analyzes data.	"Find market trends for 2025."
Execution Agent	Carries out specific tasks.	"Write a Python automation script."

Use Case: A legal firm can deploy multiple AutoGPT agents—one for **contract analysis**, another for **case law research**, and a third for **report generation**.

3. Real-World Multi-Agent Applications

Multi-agent AutoGPT setups are already transforming industries:

Finance – AI teams handle **risk assessment, fraud detection, and automated trading**.
Healthcare – Agents assist with **medical diagnosis, drug discovery, and patient management**.
E-commerce – AI-driven **product recommendations, inventory forecasting, and chatbot support**.

Example: An AI-powered news agency can assign different AutoGPT instances to:

- **Scrape news data** from multiple sources.

- **Summarize key stories** based on trends.

- **Generate publish-ready content** in multiple languages.

Conclusion

AutoGPT's architecture enables it to function **autonomously, efficiently, and intelligently**. By:

- Breaking down tasks recursively.

- Using advanced memory management.

- Coordinating multi-agent workflows.

It can revolutionize industries by automating complex workflows with minimal supervision.

Chapter 4: Advanced Customization & Integration

AutoGPT's true power lies in its flexibility and adaptability. While its default setup provides a strong foundation, professionals can **fine-tune, extend, and integrate** it into industry-specific applications.

This chapter explores:

- How to optimize AutoGPT for **finance, healthcare, and software development**.
- How to enhance AutoGPT using **APIs and custom plugins**.
- Essential **security and ethical considerations** for responsible AI deployment.

4.1 Fine-Tuning AutoGPT for Industry-Specific Needs

Different industries have unique requirements, and AutoGPT can be **customized to meet these demands**.

By adjusting its behavior, integrating domain-specific knowledge, and optimizing workflows, professionals can **maximize efficiency and accuracy**.

1. Finance and Trading Automation

AutoGPT can assist in:

Stock market predictions.

Portfolio management.

Fraud detection and compliance.

Customization Techniques:

- **Real-Time Data Feeds** – Connect AutoGPT with financial APIs (e.g., Alpha Vantage, Yahoo Finance) for up-to-date market trends.

- **Sentiment Analysis** – Use NLP techniques to analyze financial news and investor sentiment.

- **Risk Assessment Models** – Train AutoGPT on historical data to predict potential market risks.

Example: A hedge fund integrates AutoGPT with an **algorithmic trading system** that autonomously buys/sells assets based on market signals.

2. Healthcare and Medical Research Applications

AutoGPT can support medical professionals by:
Assisting with **diagnosis and treatment recommendations**.
Automating **medical literature review**.
Streamlining **drug discovery and clinical trials**.

Customization Techniques:

- **Medical Knowledge Bases** – Integrate AutoGPT with PubMed, WHO, or CDC datasets.

- **HIPAA-Compliant Data Handling** – Securely manage patient data with encryption.

- **AI-Assisted Diagnostics** – Use AutoGPT in conjunction with machine learning models trained on medical imaging.

Example: A pharmaceutical company fine-tunes AutoGPT to **analyze genetic data**, accelerating drug discovery for rare diseases.

3. Software Development Workflows

Developers can use AutoGPT for:

Code generation and debugging.

Automating DevOps tasks.

Documentation and code reviews.

Customization Techniques:

- **Integrate with GitHub/GitLab** – Allow AutoGPT to manage code repositories, review pull requests, and suggest improvements.

- **Use AI-Based Debugging** – Connect AutoGPT with error-tracking tools (e.g., Sentry, Datadog) for real-time troubleshooting.

- **Enhance Code Generation** – Train AutoGPT with a dataset of high-quality code snippets for specific frameworks (e.g., React, Django, Node.js).

Example: A software company deploys AutoGPT to **automatically refactor legacy code**, improving performance while ensuring compliance with modern best practices.

4.2 API Extensions and Plugins

AutoGPT becomes significantly more powerful when integrated with **external APIs and third-party tools**.

1. Integrating External APIs

By connecting AutoGPT with APIs, it can:

- Retrieve real-time data (weather, finance, news).

- Automate customer support with CRM tools.

- Access cloud storage for document processing.

Examples of Useful APIs:

- **Google Cloud AI** – Advanced NLP and vision capabilities.

- **OpenAI API** – Access GPT-4 for specialized tasks.

- **Twilio API** – Automate SMS/email notifications.

- **Stripe API** – Enable automated financial transactions.

Example: A marketing agency links AutoGPT with Google Analytics to generate **AI-driven campaign performance reports**.

2. Enhancing AutoGPT with Third-Party Tools

AutoGPT can be extended with tools like: **LangChain** – Improves AI memory and reasoning. **Pinecone** – Enhances long-term vector memory. **Zapier** – Automates task workflows with hundreds of integrations.

Example: A business automates HR processes by integrating AutoGPT with **Notion for employee tracking and Slack for notifications**.

3. Creating Custom Plugins

For **maximum control and functionality**, professionals can develop custom plugins tailored to their specific needs.

- **Why Create Plugins?**

- Extend AutoGPT with **custom data processing**.
- Improve **task execution speed**.
- Connect with **proprietary databases and software**.

- **How to Build a Plugin?**

1-**Define the plugin's function** (e.g., scraping real estate listings, parsing legal documents).

2-**Use Python to develop it** (AutoGPT supports Python-based plugins).

3-**Integrate with AutoGPT** via API calls or local execution.

4-**Test and optimize** performance.

Example: A legal firm builds a **contract analysis plugin** for AutoGPT, allowing it to scan legal documents, identify risks, and summarize key clauses.

4.3 Security and Ethical Considerations

While AutoGPT offers incredible potential, **security risks and ethical challenges** must be addressed to ensure responsible AI deployment.

1. Data Privacy Concerns

Potential Risks:

✓ Exposure of sensitive user data.

✓ Unauthorized data retention.

✓ API security vulnerabilities.

- **Best Practices for Data Security:**

- Use **end-to-end encryption** for sensitive data.

- Implement **role-based access controls (RBAC)**.

- Regularly audit API calls and **monitor for anomalies**.

Example: A healthcare AI firm integrates AutoGPT **with strict access controls**, ensuring only authorized personnel can view medical records.

2. Bias Mitigation Strategies

AutoGPT, like all AI models, can inherit **biases from its training data**.

Common Bias Issues:
Skewed recommendations based on incomplete datasets.
Unfair treatment of different demographics.
Inaccurate financial or medical predictions.

- **How to Reduce Bias:**

- Train AutoGPT on **diverse, representative datasets**.

- Implement **AI explainability techniques** to track decision-making.

- Regularly test for **algorithmic bias** and adjust model weights.

Example: A recruitment firm using AutoGPT for **resume screening** ensures fairness by **training it on anonymized, unbiased hiring data**.

3. Compliance with AI Regulations

Companies must ensure their AI implementations **comply with global regulations**:

📋 **Key AI Regulations to Consider:**

- **GDPR (Europe)** – Protects user data privacy.
- **CCPA (California)** – Governs personal data use.
- **AI Act (EU Proposal)** – Aims to regulate high-risk AI systems.
- **HIPAA (USA)** – Protects patient health data.

- **How to Ensure Compliance:**

- Keep records of **AI decision-making processes**.

- Use **consent-based data collection** practices.

- Conduct **regular security audits** to prevent misuse.

Example: A fintech startup integrating AutoGPT with **customer loan approvals** ensures **regulatory compliance** by logging all AI-driven financial decisions.

Conclusion

AutoGPT can be **fine-tuned and expanded** for almost any industry, offering unparalleled automation and intelligence.

By:

- **Customizing industry-specific workflows**.

- **Integrating powerful APIs and plugins**.

- **Prioritizing security, bias mitigation, and compliance**.

Professionals can **deploy AutoGPT responsibly and efficiently**.

Chapter 5: Case Studies & Real-World Applications

AutoGPT is transforming industries by automating complex workflows, improving efficiency, and enabling data-driven decision-making. This chapter explores **real-world use cases** where AutoGPT has been successfully deployed across **business, software development, and research**.

By examining these **case studies**, you'll gain **actionable insights** into how AutoGPT can be tailored to meet your specific needs.

5.1 Business Process Automation

Businesses are leveraging AutoGPT to automate repetitive tasks, streamline operations, and **enhance decision-making**. From market research to customer support, AI-driven automation can reduce costs and improve efficiency.

Case Study: AI-Powered Market Research

Challenge: A digital marketing agency struggled with manually collecting and analyzing consumer insights. Their team spent **dozens of hours** each week researching trends, competitors, and customer sentiment.

Solution: The agency integrated **AutoGPT with web scraping tools and sentiment analysis APIs** to:

- Automatically gather **real-time consumer insights** from social media and forums.

- Generate **trend reports** based on customer feedback.

- Summarize competitors' **marketing strategies and campaign performance**.

Outcome:

- Research time reduced by **80%**.

- Improved **customer targeting and campaign performance**.

- **Faster, data-driven decision-making** for marketing strategies.

Example *Workflow:*

1-AutoGPT scrapes product reviews and social media discussions.

2-It uses NLP techniques to **identify positive/negative sentiment**.

3-The AI generates **a summary report** with key insights and recommended actions.

Automating Customer Support with AutoGPT

Challenge: A growing e-commerce company struggled with handling a high volume of customer inquiries. Their support team was overwhelmed, leading to **delayed responses and poor customer satisfaction**.

Solution: AutoGPT was deployed as a **smart chatbot** integrated with the company's CRM and ticketing system. It could:

- **Automatically respond to common inquiries** (e.g., order status, refunds).

- Escalate complex issues to human agents **only when necessary**.

- Learn from past interactions to **improve response accuracy over time**.

 Outcome:
- **Customer wait times reduced by 60%**.
- **24/7 support availability**, increasing global reach.
- Human agents **focused on high-priority issues**, improving overall service quality.

 Example Workflow:
1-AutoGPT scans incoming support tickets and classifies them by **urgency and topic**.
2-It retrieves relevant answers from the **company's knowledge base**.
3-It interacts with customers via **email, chat, or voice assistant**.

5.2 Software Development & DevOps

AutoGPT is also revolutionizing **software engineering** by automating repetitive tasks, improving code quality, and optimizing DevOps workflows.

Case Study: Automated Bug Tracking

Challenge: A software company faced delays due to **inefficient bug tracking**. Developers manually reviewed logs and error reports, slowing down the debugging process.

Solution: The company integrated AutoGPT with their **error monitoring system (Sentry, Datadog)** to:
- **Automatically detect and categorize bugs** based on error logs.
- Suggest potential **root causes and fixes**.
- Prioritize bugs based on **user impact and frequency**.

Outcome:
- Debugging time reduced by **50%**.

- Fewer production issues, improving **software reliability**.
- Increased **developer productivity**.

Example Workflow:

1-AutoGPT scans **error logs** and categorizes bugs (e.g., UI glitches, backend failures).

2-It cross-references code changes to **identify likely causes**.

3-It suggests fixes and **notifies developers** with relevant documentation.

AutoGPT-Assisted Code Refactoring

Challenge: A fintech startup had a **large legacy codebase** that was difficult to maintain. Developers struggled to update the code while ensuring security and performance.

Solution: The team deployed AutoGPT to:

- Analyze the codebase and **identify redundant or inefficient code**.

- Suggest **optimized, more maintainable alternatives**.

- Automatically **refactor repetitive code patterns** to improve readability and security.

Outcome:

- **30% reduction** in code complexity.
- **Faster onboarding** for new developers due to cleaner code.
- **Better performance and security** without breaking existing functionality.

Example Workflow:

1-AutoGPT scans the repository and identifies **duplicate code and inefficiencies**.

2-It recommends **optimized functions** and **code modularization strategies**.

3-Developers review and **approve/refine** the AI-generated changes.

5.3 Research & Content Generation

AutoGPT is transforming knowledge work by **automating literature reviews, summarizing complex research, and enhancing content strategies**.

Case Study: AI-Generated Scientific Literature Review

Challenge: A university research team needed to review **hundreds of academic papers** on machine learning advancements, but manual summarization was too time-consuming.

Solution: The team trained AutoGPT to:
- **Search and extract** relevant papers from arXiv, PubMed, and IEEE Xplore.
- Summarize key findings, methodologies, and limitations.
- Organize information **into structured reports** with citations.

Outcome:

- Researchers saved **weeks of manual reading**.

- Literature reviews became **more comprehensive and up-to-date**.

- Faster discovery of **research gaps and opportunities**.

Example Workflow:

1-AutoGPT **scrapes academic databases** for relevant papers.

2-It extracts **abstracts, methodologies, and key conclusions**.

3-It generates a **concise research summary** with citation links.

Enhancing Content Strategy with AutoGPT

Challenge: A content marketing team struggled to **produce high-quality blog posts** at scale while keeping up with SEO trends.

Solution: AutoGPT was used to:

- Generate **SEO-optimized content outlines** based on

trending keywords.

- Suggest **article structures, headings, and meta descriptions**.

- Assist in **rewording and improving readability**.

Outcome:

- **Content production doubled** without increasing staff workload.

- **Improved search rankings**, leading to more organic traffic.

- Writers focused more on **creativity and storytelling**, while AI handled research and structuring.

Example Workflow:

1-AutoGPT analyzes search trends and **suggests high-ranking topics**.

2-It generates **detailed content outlines** with key points.

3-Writers refine AI-generated drafts into **engaging, polished articles**.

Conclusion

From business automation to research and software development, AutoGPT is **reshaping industries**.

- It **automates repetitive tasks**, freeing up human expertise for strategic work.
- It **enhances productivity** by accelerating research, debugging, and content creation.
- It **reduces costs and improves efficiency** for businesses of all sizes.

Chapter 6: Troubleshooting & Best Practices

Even with its advanced capabilities, AutoGPT is not **perfect**—it can produce **hallucinations, inefficient responses, or high API costs** if not properly optimized. This chapter focuses on **troubleshooting common issues**, **performance optimization**, and **future trends** in autonomous AI.

6.1 Common Pitfalls and How to Avoid Them

Despite AutoGPT's power, users often encounter **three major challenges**:

1-**Hallucinations (AI Generating False or Misleading Information)**
2-**Excessive Token Usage & High API Costs**
3-**Task Execution Errors and Failures**

Handling Hallucinations in AI Responses

Problem:

AutoGPT sometimes **"hallucinates"**—generating responses that sound plausible but are **factually incorrect or irrelevant**.

Solution:

- **Enable external verification** – Integrate web search or database lookups.

- **Use grounding techniques** – Feed AutoGPT with structured data or reference materials.

- **Limit response creativity** – Adjust temperature settings (lower values = more factual).

- **Cross-check AI outputs** – Human review is essential for critical applications.

Example Fix:

Instead of allowing **free-text generation**, restrict AI responses to **pre-defined knowledge sources**, improving accuracy.

Optimizing Token Usage and API Costs

Problem:

AutoGPT can quickly **consume API tokens**, leading to **unexpected high costs**.

Solution:

- **Set response length limits** – Use max_tokens to prevent excessive output.

- **Use caching mechanisms** – Store previous responses to avoid repeated API calls.

- **Leverage local models** – If cost is a concern, deploy **open-source models** (e.g., GPT4All, DeepSeek).

- **Optimize prompt engineering** – Reduce redundant input text for efficiency.

Example   *Fix:*

Instead of sending **full conversation history** with every request, use a **summary of previous interactions** to reduce token usage.

6.2 Performance Optimization Tips

To maximize AutoGPT's efficiency, consider the following **best practices**.

Improving Response Efficiency

🪁 Use Parallel Processing

Instead of sequential tasks, run multiple AutoGPT instances in **parallel**.

⚡ Prioritize Important Queries

Set **confidence thresholds** to ignore low-value responses and focus on **high-impact answers**.

∞ Use Vector Databases for Memory

Instead of raw text storage, use **FAISS, Pinecone, or ChromaDB** for faster recall.

Example Fix:

Instead of making AutoGPT process **entire datasets** repeatedly, let it **fetch only relevant sections** using vector search.

Scaling AutoGPT for Enterprise Use

For large-scale deployments, **performance bottlenecks** can arise.

Solution:

- **Use cloud-based models** – Deploy on **AWS, GCP, or Azure** for scalability.

- **Implement load balancing** – Distribute requests across multiple instances.

- **Monitor AI workflows** – Track AutoGPT's efficiency using logging tools like **Prometheus**.

Example Fix:

A company deploying **AutoGPT for customer support** can **distribute the workload across multiple GPUs to handle thousands of queries simultaneously**.

6.3 Future of AutoGPT and Autonomous AI

Upcoming Developments in AI Autonomy

Memory-Enhanced Models

Future versions of AutoGPT will **store long-term memory**, reducing repetitive learning.

Self-Improving AI Agents

AI will **learn from its mistakes** and improve **without human intervention**.

Multi-Agent Collaboration

AutoGPT could work **alongside other AI models**, each with **specialized roles**.

Predictions for AI-Assisted Workflows

More Human-AI Hybrid Workflows

AI will **automate repetitive tasks**, while humans **focus on creativity & decision-making**.

AI Will Handle Entire Business Operations

From **finance to customer service**, autonomous AI will become **a core part of enterprises**.

Example Scenario:

A **fully autonomous AI CEO** managing a small business with **minimal human intervention**.

By understanding **common pitfalls, optimization strategies, and future trends**, you can unlock AutoGPT's **full potential**.

Conclusion: Mastering AutoGPT for the Future

AutoGPT is more than just another AI tool—it represents a **paradigm shift** in how professionals approach **automation, problem-solving, and efficiency**. By leveraging **autonomous AI agents**, businesses and individuals can **streamline workflows, accelerate decision-making, and unlock new levels of productivity**.

Why Mastering AutoGPT Matters

Stay ahead of the AI revolution – As AI rapidly evolves, those who understand and harness its power will lead the future.

Automate complex tasks – From business operations to software development, AutoGPT simplifies processes that once required **extensive human effort**.

Enhance decision-making – With its ability to

analyze data, iterate solutions, and adapt, AutoGPT serves as an **intelligent assistant** for professionals.

Beyond This Guidebook: Your Next Steps

- **Experiment with AutoGPT in real-world applications** – Start small, then scale your projects as you gain experience.
- **Customize and optimize AI workflows** – Fine-tune models to fit **your industry-specific needs**.
- **Stay updated with AI advancements** – The field of **autonomous agents** is evolving rapidly—continuous learning will keep you at the forefront.

Table of Contents :

www.ingramcontent.com/pod-product-compliance
Lightning Source LLC
La Vergne TN
LVHW051614050326
832903LV00033B/4493